By Theresa Morin
Illustrations by Ron Wheeler

Esther was a very beautiful young woman, the prettiest in all the land. One day she was summoned to the king's castle.

"Hurry, Esther, the king is looking for a wife to be his queen," the servant said. "And you have been chosen!"

When the king saw Esther come toward his throne, he fell in love. He had never seen such a beautiful, graceful woman!

The king set the royal crown on her head and made her the new queen. Then he gave a big party so everyone could meet Queen Esther.

Esther was happy to be queen. She was full of goodness, wisdom, and grace, and all the people in the kingdom loved her.

But then she received bad news from her uncle Mordecai. Prince Haman was planning to hurt the Jews, God's special people. And Uncle Mordecai and Queen Esther were Jews!

"You have to help our people, Queen Esther,"
begged Uncle Mordecai. "You are the only one
the king really listens to. Tell him you and I are
Jews, too."

Queen Esther was scared. Such a big favor to ask the king! Did she dare ask him? What if he said no?

But Queen Esther loved her uncle Mordecai—he had raised her since she was orphaned as a little girl. She prayed to God for courage—and then she felt herself becoming brave.

Queen Esther knew the right thing to do was to persuade the king to help the Jews. "Yes, of course I'll help our people," she promised.

Queen Esther put on her prettiest gown and slowly walked toward the throne.

The king gave her permission to come nearer to him. "What is your wish, Queen Esther?" he asked. "I will give it to you even if it is half my kingdom."

"Please, Your Highness," began Esther. "A bad man is planning to hurt my people, the Jews. I beg you to stop him and save us all."

The King was angry that someone would plan to hurt his beloved queen and her people. He promised he would rescue them and keep them safe!

Uncle Mordecai was happy that Queen Esther
had persuaded the king to save the Jews. She was
so brave and smart!

Uncle Mordecai made sure every Jew in the country knew what Queen Esther had done. He told everyone about her courage.

"Long live Queen Esther!" the people shouted.
They danced and sang and ate lots of good food
to celebrate their safety.

They named their celebration Purim, and to this day Jewish people around the world enjoy the holiday in honor of what Queen Esther did for them.

Queen Esther had always wanted to serve God.
And she had the chance to do something good
and helpful.